The Cat in the Hat's Learning Library
T0015920

To Alyce and Pat, with love.
—T.R.

The editors would like to thank
BARBARA KIEFER, Ph.D.,
Charlotte S. Huck Professor of Children's Literature,
The Ohio State University, and
KATHERINE MADIN, Ph.D.,
Curriculum Coordinator, Woods Hole Oceanographic Institution,
for their assistance in the preparation of this book.

TM & copyright © by Dr. Seuss Enterprises, L.P. 2005
THE CAT IN THE HAT'S LEARNING LIBRARY logos and word mark are registered trademarks of Dr. Seuss Enterprises, L.P.
THE CAT IN THE HAT'S LEARNING LIBRARY logos © Dr. Seuss Enterprises, L.P. 1998

THE CAT IN THE HAT KNOWS A LOT ABOUT THAT! logo and word mark TM 2010 Dr. Seuss Enterprises, L.P., Portfolio Entertainment, Inc., and Collingwood O'Hare Productions, Ltd. All rights reserved. The PBS KIDS logo is a registered trademark of PBS. Both are used with permission. All rights reserved.

All rights reserved. Published in the United States by Random House Children's Books, a division of Penguin Random House LLC, New York.

Random House and the colophon are registered trademarks of Penguin Random House LLC.

Visit us on the Web!
Seussville.com
rhcbooks.com

Educators and librarians, for a variety of teaching tools, visit us at
RHTeachersLibrarians.com

Library of Congress Cataloging-in-Publication Data
Rabe, Tish.
Clam-I-Am! : all about the beach / by Tish Rabe ; illustrated by Aristides Ruiz and Joe Mathieu.
p. cm. — (The Cat in the Hat's learning library)
ISBN 978-0-375-82280-3 (trade) — ISBN 978-0-593-12655-4 (ebook)
1. Seashore biology—Juvenile literature. 2. Beachcombing—Juvenile literature.
3. Ocean—Juvenile literature. I. Ruiz, Aristides, ill. II. Mathieu, Joe, ill. III. Title. IV. Series.
QH95.7.R24 2005 578.769'9—dc22 2004014613

MANUFACTURED IN CHINA
50 49 48 47 46 45 44 43 42 41 40 39 38 37 36 35

Random House Children's Books supports the First Amendment and celebrates the right to read.

Clam-I-Am!

by Tish Rabe

illustrated by Aristides Ruiz and Joe Mathieu

The Cat in the Hat's Learning Library®

Random House New York

Hello! I'm the Fish.
To the beach let us go!
The Fish Channel asked me
to star in a show.

It is called *Fish and Friends*.
You can be in it, too.
Your mother will not
mind at all if you do.

Today on our show
we are off to explore
where the sea meets the sand
at the edge of the shore.

Here where the waves crash
in bubbles of foam,
you'll meet lots of creatures
who call the beach home.

Meet my friend Clam-I-Am!
She would like to say, "Hi."
She lives in the sand.
She's a little bit shy.

Clam-I-Am has two shells.
They have rings, you see here.
Rings show how much
she has grown every year.

See this hole in the sand? Well, Thing One and I know it means there's a clam in the sand down below.
A clam has one foot that helps it move about. Clams pull salt water in and spit salt water out!

Hello, horseshoe crab!
How did he get his name?
His shell and a horseshoe
are both shaped the same.

His shell shields his body
from any attack.
His eyes are in front.
His tail is in back.

He has four eyes
but can't see very well.
To find food, he is helped
by his keen sense of smell.
2
4
1
3
They are not really crabs!
Every crab has an-TEN-nee.
Look closely, you'll see
horseshoe "crabs" don't have any!

Hermit crabs don't have shells,
so they look till they find
empty shells on the sand
that have been left behind.

Then they drag these new shells
everywhere that they go.
When the shells get too tight,
they need more room to grow.

So each crab starts to hunt
for a new shell to use.
There are lots to be found.
It is easy to choose!

My next guest is a sea star!
He told me today
that each of his five legs
is known as a ray.

If a sea star gets hurt
and it loses a ray,
a new ray begins
to grow back right away.

Sea stars are quite slow
when they move around.
Tiny cups on their feet
hold them on to the ground.
These creatures are mollusks.
Most have a hard shell.
Shells protect their soft bodies—
and do it quite well.

Seaweed doesn't have roots.
It grabs rocks, then holds tight.
Some seaweed grows up,
where it gets the sun's light.

Some seaweed you'll find
grows a lot deeper down.
Seaweed can be green,
purple, red, pink, or brown.

When you pick seaweed up, you'll find creatures like these. They're sand hoppers, which are also known as sand fleas.

Seagulls fly near the ocean.
Their cries fill the air.
If you're eating your lunch,
they are hoping you'll share.
We learned this about seagulls.
Would you ever think it?
Seawater is salty,
but seagulls can drink it!

They're not fussy eaters.
They think it's a treat
if they find some dead fish
or some garbage to eat.
SUN BLOCK
Juice
Sandpipers run with
the waves at low tide.
They search with their bills
to find worms where they hide.

Spend time on the beach and you'll see right away the ocean has high and low tides every day.

Tides are caused by the sun and the moon, and I know their forces pull the oceans and make the tides flow.

At low tide the water pulls back from the shore.

At high tide it is back where it started before.
SEUSSVILLE U.S.A.
AUG. 8
HIGH TIDE 12:47AM 4.48ft.
LOW TIDE 7:19AM 0.58ft.
HIGH TIDE 2:22 PM 4.36ft.
LOW TIDE 7:50 PM 2.36ft.
A tide table like this makes it easy to see when today's two low tides and two high tides will be.

If you walk on the beach at low tide, you will find all kinds of sea creatures the tide left behind.
See these clear blobs of jelly? Thing Two and I fear them. Some jellyfish sting! So we do not go near them!
THING

Some shells travel miles
and miles without breaking.
Find a shell in one piece and
you know it's worth taking!
Find a big shell like this.
Put it up to your ear.
You might be surprised
by the sounds that you hear!

This tidal pool
you will find is a home
to creatures who stay here
and who never roam.

These shells are called barnacles.
Watch them right here.

When a wave washes over them, threads will appear.
These threads are the barnacle's feathery feet. They grab food floating by for this creature to eat.
Not far from the shore, sand is blown into dunes. Dunes are home to crabs, birds, rabbits, mice, and raccoons.

When we go to the beach,
we make sure that we take
some old sneakers,
a pail,
a small net,
and a rake.

We wear our old sneakers
without any socks
so our feet won't get cut
by glass, shells, or rocks.

A net lets us scoop things
out of the sea.
A rake helps us dig
in the sand easily.

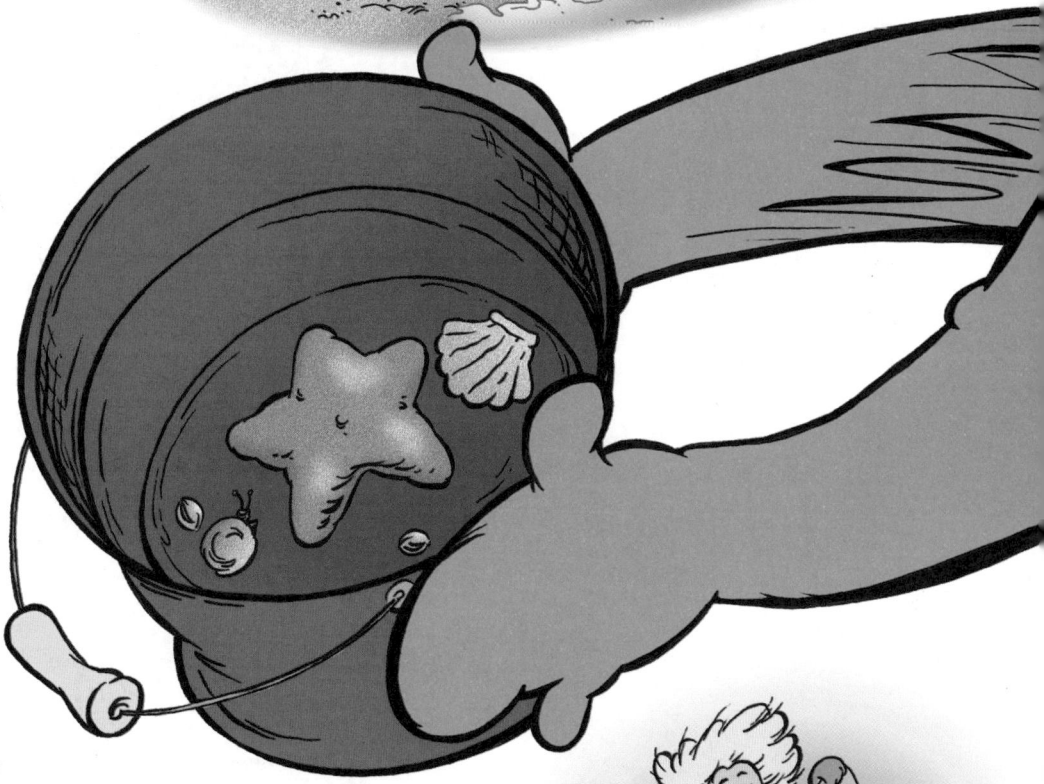

We put what we find
in our pail and then, when
it is time to go home,
set them free once again!

The next part of my show
I call "Go Ask the Fish."
I will answer three questions.
Pick one, if you wish.

Ocean water is clear,
it just LOOKS blue. Here's why—

like a mirror, it shines back
the blue from the sky.

If you look at the ocean
on a dark, cloudy day,
it shines back the clouds,
so the water looks gray.

Raindrops fall from the sky
and fill rivers, which flow,
washing salt off rocks
wherever they go.

Rivers flow to the ocean,
and as the years pass,

some water heats up
and is turned into gas.

The salt in the water
is left, and that's why
oceans get saltier
as time passes by.

Wind blows over water,
and small waves then grow.

They get bigger and bigger
the stronger winds blow.

They keep going and growing
and head toward the land.
Then the waves hit the beach,
and they crash on the sand.

When the strong winds die down,
then the waves die down, too.
Until the next time when
the wind blows on through.

Next, it's "Shop with the Fish"!
We have gifts from the sea!
You can order today,
and the gifts are all free!
MESSAGE IN A BOTTLE
We have pieces of sea glass.
The sun makes them glow!
They are pieces of bottles
that broke long ago.
SEA SHELLS

They were tossed by the waves.
Over time, they were ground
by the salt and the sand
till the edges were round.
I've got lots of sea glass
and most of it's green.
This piece is the prettiest
I've ever seen.

We have beautiful driftwood,
and here's the best part—
it's ready-made sculpture,
real pieces of art!

Tossed by the wind
and the waves every day,
it was bleached by the sun
till it turned a light gray.

To make this wind chime,
I took lots of shells
and hung them together.
They jingle like bells.
To make this sand painting,
first take colored sand,
then, for the patterns,
let it fall from your hand.
STARFISH
THING 2

Oh dear, our show's over.
We must hit the road.
Please join us next time
for a new episode.

Come back to the beach.
You will smell the salt air,
hear the cry of the gull,
feel the wind in your hair.

You will find a seashell
to hold in your hand,
build a high castle,
dig your toes in the sand.

Everywhere that you look
you'll find creatures galore.
When you look even closer,
you'll find . . .

even more!

GLOSSARY

Antennae: A pair of long feelers used to sense touch and smells.

Barnacle: A tiny animal with a hard shell that attaches itself to rocks and other objects.

Bleached: Removed of color; lightened; whitened.

Jellyfish: A sea animal with a body that is soft like jelly, is shaped like an umbrella, and has tentacles to sting its prey.

Keen: Sharp in sensing.

Mollusk: An animal with a soft body and no backbone.

Sand flea: A small hopping animal related to shrimp that lives in dry seaweed on the beach.

Sculpture: A molded or carved work of art.

Shield: To defend or protect.

Tentacles: Long, thin body parts used to feel, grasp, or sting.

FOR FURTHER READING

Follow the Water from Brook to Ocean by Arthur Dorros (HarperCollins, *Let's-Read-and-Find-Out Science*®, Stage 2). Learn where water comes from, how it gets to the ocean, and what happens to it after that. For kindergarten and up.

High Tide for Horseshoe Crabs by Lisa Kahn Schnell, illustrated by Alan Marks (Charlesbridge). An excellent introduction to horseshoe crabs and their annual spawning in Delaware Bay. For preschool–grade 2.

On My Beach There Are Many Pebbles by Leo Lionni (HarperCollins). A simple story with wonderful illustrations showing the countless pebbles waiting to be discovered. For preschool and up.

Seashore, with photos by Steve Parker (Dorling Kindersley, *Eyewitness Books*). Incredible photographs show all varieties of life found on the beach. For grades 4 and up.

What Makes an Ocean Wave? Questions and Answers About Oceans and Ocean Life by Melvin and Gilda Berger, illustrated by John Rice (Scholastic). All about oceans and ocean life. For grades 3 and up.

INDEX

barnacles, 26–27
beach, 8, 22, 24, 28, 35, 40
birds, 20–21, 27

clams, 10–11
crabs, 12–15, 27

driftwood, 38
dunes, 27

hermit crabs, 14–15
horseshoe crabs, 12–13

jellyfish, 24

mollusks, 17

sand, 8, 10, 11, 14, 27, 35, 37, 39, 41
sand hoppers (sand fleas), 19
sandpipers, 21
sea glass, 36–37
seagulls, 20–21, 40
sea stars, 16–17
seawater, 11
  color of, 31
  saltiness of, 20, 32–33
seaweed, 18–19
shells, 10, 12, 14–15, 17, 25, 28, 39, 41

tidal pools, 26–27
tides, 21, 22–23, 24
tide table, 23

waves, 8, 21, 27, 34–35, 37, 38
wind, 34–35, 38, 40

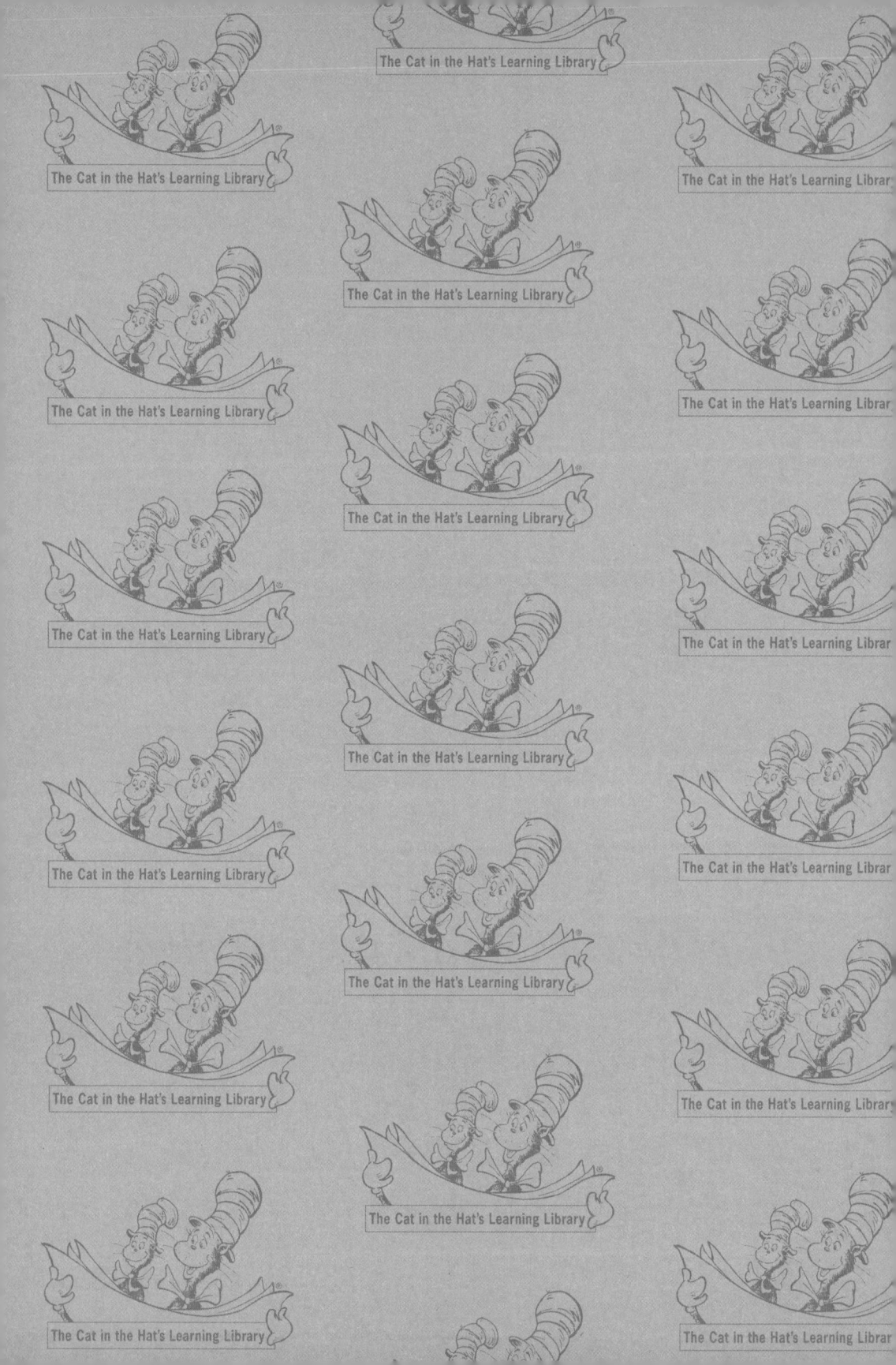
The Cat in the Hat's Learning Library